Reading Comprehension

Written by **Michelle Thompson**

Illustrations by **Clive Scruton**

FlashKids

An imprint of Sterling Children's Books

This book belongs to

_____

FLASH KIDS, STERLING, and the distinctive Sterling logo are registered trademarks of
Sterling Publishing Co., Inc.

Published by Sterling Publishing Co., Inc.
387 Park Avenue South, New York, NY 10016
Text and illustrations © 2006 by Flash Kids
Distributed in Canada by Sterling Publishing
c/o Canadian Manda Group, 165 Dufferin Street
Toronto, Ontario, Canada M6K 3H6
Distributed in the United Kingdom by GMC Distribution Services
Castle Place, 166 High Street, Lewes, East Sussex, England BN7 1XU
Distributed in Australia by Capricorn Link (Australia) Pty. Ltd.
P.O. Box 704, Windsor, NSW 2756, Australia

Sterling ISBN 978-1-4114-3446-2

Manufactured in Canada

Lot #:
10 12 14 15 13 11
04/13

For information about custom editions, special sales, premium and
corporate purchases, please contact Sterling Special Sales
Department at 800-805-5489 or specialsales@sterlingpublishing.com.

Cover design and production by Mada Design, Inc.

Dear Parent,

Once young children have learned to read, the next important step is to make sure that they understand and retain the information they encounter. The passages and activities contained in this book will provide your child with plenty of opportunities to develop these vital reading comprehension skills. The more your child reads and responds to literature, the greater the improvement you will see in his or her mastery of reading comprehension. To get the most from *Reading Comprehension*, follow these simple steps:

- Find a comfortable place where you and your child can work quietly together.
- Encourage your child to work at his or her own pace.
- Help your child read the words and sentences, and ask questions about the content of what he or she has read.
- Offer lots of praise and support.
- Let your child reward his or her work with the included stickers.
- Most of all, remember that learning should be fun! Take time to look at the pictures, laugh at the funny characters, and enjoy this special time spent together.

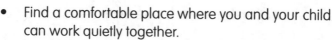

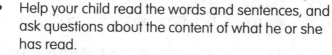

Take Me Out to the Ball Game

Every year, baseball fans in the United States look forward to the opening day of the major-league baseball season. In an act of tradition, the President of the United States throws out the "first pitch" of the season at the start of this game. This practice has not always been a part of professional baseball, but it now serves as a yearly reminder that baseball is one of America's favorite hobbies.

On April 4, 1910, U.S. President William Howard Taft proudly began this special tradition. As a boy, Taft enjoyed playing baseball. He felt that the sport drew crowds of people who liked "clean, straight athletics." Since this historic game between Philadelphia and Washington, each new president has warmed up his pitching arm and tossed out the ball that began the next season.

Answer the questions.

1. What do baseball fans look forward to each year?

   Major league baseball seasen.

2. Who throws out the first pitch of the season?

   _____

3. On what date did this tradition begin?

   _____

4. Who was the first president to begin this tradition?

   _____

5. Which teams were playing during this game?

   _____

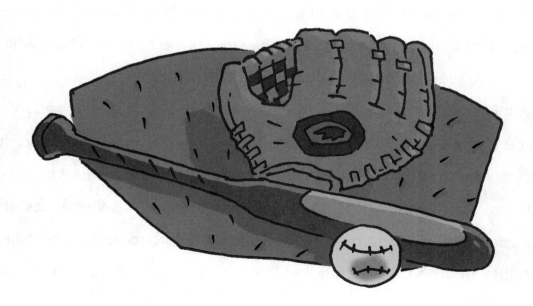

National Anthem

Have you ever listened to the words of the U.S. national anthem? The lyrics, or words to the song, were written by Francis Scott Key. Key wrote the words after watching a battle between British and American forces during the War of 1812. The song tells the story of the American flag, which continued to wave through the fighting of that night.

By the early 1900s, during World War I, the U.S. Army began to use the song as a patriotic war song. The popular tune and powerful words soon caught on with the rest of the country. However, the song, titled the "Star-Spangled Banner," was not officially adopted as the American national anthem until 1931. To this day, proud Americans stand when they hear the "Star-Spangled Banner" as a sign of respect, loyalty, and patriotism.

Fill in the blanks with the correct answers.

1. The U.S. national anthem is called the

   _____ .

2. _____

   wrote the lyrics to the national anthem.

3. Key wrote the words after watching a battle between British and

   American forces during the War of _____ .

4. The anthem became popular in the early _____ .

5. The song was adopted as the U.S. national anthem in _____ .

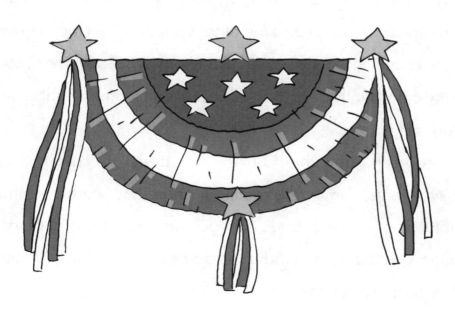

Spelling Bees

Spelling contests, or spelling bees, got their start in the late 1700s when Benjamin Franklin suggested that teachers encourage excellence in spelling. Students were paired together to quiz each other until one student misspelled a word and the other was declared the winner. These spelling contests first began inside schoolhouses. They later made their way into the community because parents, friends, and neighbors came to watch students compete.

These contests became known as "bees" because they were community events, similar to quilting bees and corn-husking bees. The popularity of spelling bees spread throughout the country. Today, the tradition continues, as students compete in school, city, state, and national-level spelling bees!

Answer the questions.

1. What are competitions in spelling called?

   _____

2. When did these competitions get their start?

   _____

3. Who suggested that teachers encourage excellence in spelling?

   _____

4. Who attended spelling contests that were held in the community?

   _____

   _____

5. What other community events were similar to these spelling contests

   in the community?

   _____

   _____

Cotton Candy

For over 100 years, people have enjoyed the taste of cotton candy. Cotton candy is made from pure melted sugar. The cotton candy machine, invented by Thomas Patton, spins the melted sugar, pushing liquid through small holes in the machine. As the sugar passes through the holes, it is cooled and shaped into long threads. The threads are gathered onto a stick or paper cone. First introduced at the Ringling Bros. circus in 1900, cotton candy has been a common treat found at circuses, fairs, and carnivals across the country.

Fill in the blanks. Then write the answers in the puzzle.

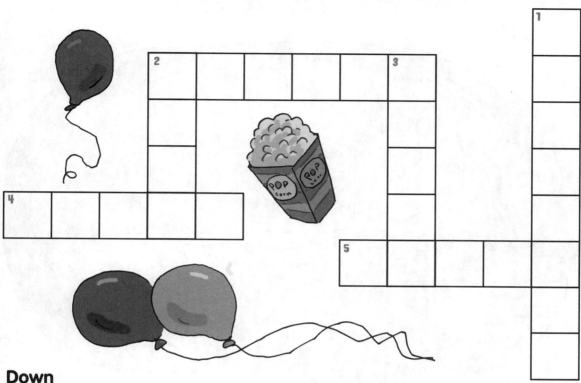

Down

1. Thomas Patton _____ the cotton candy machine.

2. The cotton candy is gathered onto a stick or paper _____.

3. Cotton candy is made from pure melted _____.

Across

2. Cotton candy was introduced in 1900 at the Ringling Bros.

   _____.

4. The machine spins the sugar and pushes it through small

   _____.

5. Cotton candy is a favorite _____ at carnivals and fairs.

Hurricanes

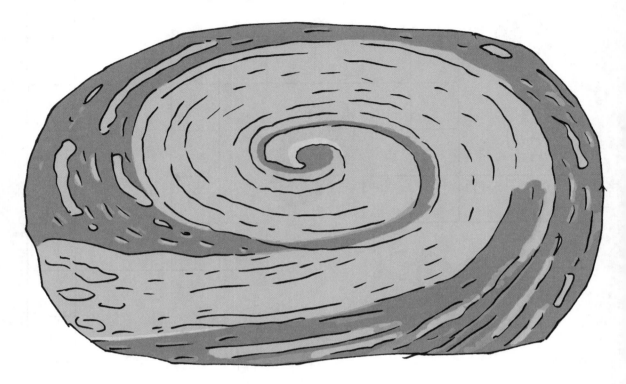

Hurricanes begin as tropical storms over the warm Atlantic Ocean. Once the winds of a tropical storm reach 75 miles per hour, the National Hurricane Center names it a hurricane. As these winds pick up speed, they swirl around the "eye," or center, of the storm. The eye of a hurricane is surprisingly calm and cloudless. Just outside the eye of the storm, thick clouds form to create a wall around the center of the hurricane. The powerful force of the wind that is created by a hurricane can reach up to 300 miles outside of the eye of the storm. This can create a lot of damage to objects in a hurricane's path!

Read each statement. Write true or false.

1. Tropical storms begin as hurricanes. _____

2. Hurricanes form over the Atlantic Ocean. _____

3. A storm is called a hurricane once winds
   reach 300 miles per hour. _____

4. The center of a hurricane is called the "eye." _____

5. There are no clouds in the eye of a hurricane. _____

Delightful Dolphins

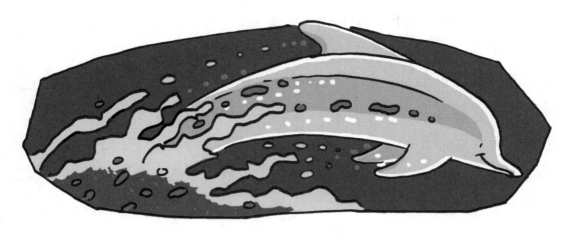

Dolphins are amazing ocean animals. Weighing up to 450 pounds and measuring up to 13 feet in length, dolphins are mammals that need air to survive. Every 15 minutes or so, dolphins rise to the water's surface to take in air from a blowhole on the top of their bodies. To continue breathing and prevent drowning while they sleep, dolphins doze with only half of their brains! They close one eye and nap near the surface of the water, swimming slowly and coming up for air. This is called "logging" because the slow-moving dolphins look like floating logs.

While there are about 40 different kinds of dolphins, each uses a special sound-locating ability called echolocation to find food in the water. Dolphins send out sounds that bounce off objects and come back as echoes. Dolphins also "talk" to each other through a series of clicking sounds or pulses of up to 300 sounds per second.

Read the statements on the dolphins.
Circle the dolphins with statements that are true.

Dolphins are mammals.

Dolphins sleep on the ocean floor.

Dolphins use echolocation to find food.

Dolphins measure up to 35 feet in length.

Dolphins "talk" to each other using clicking sounds.

At the Drive-In

In the 1930s, going to the movies was a favorite activity for adults. They would get a babysitter for the children, get dressed up, and go downtown to the movie theater on a weekend evening. Then one man had an idea for making movie-going easy and fun for families.

On June 6, 1933, Richard M. Hollingshead, Jr., and three partners opened the first drive-in movie theater. For an admission price of only 25¢ per car, families could drive to the theater, park in front of a large screen, and enjoy the movie without ever leaving their automobiles! Soon, other drive-in movie theaters began popping up all over the country.

While drive-in theaters are hard to find today, they changed the way people view movies. Now, instead of being for adults only, movie-going is something everyone can enjoy!

Answer the questions.

1. For whom was movie-going a favorite activity in the 1930s?

   _____

2. When did the first drive-in movie theater open?

   _____

3. Who was the inventor of the drive-in movie theater?

   _____

4. What was the admission price of the first drive-in movie theater?

   _____

5. After drive-in movie theaters opened, what changed about the way

   people see movies?_____

   _____

Our Solar System

In science class, Mark built a model of our solar system. First, Mark selected Styrofoam balls in different sizes to use as planets. In books from the library, Mark found pictures of the nine planets. Then he painted the Styrofoam balls to match the pictures of the planets. He painted the largest Styrofoam ball yellow to look like the sun. Next, Mark poked nine different sticks into the big yellow ball and connected each of the smaller balls, one on each stick. Finally, using a marker, Mark labeled the balls with the name of the planets: Mercury, Venus, Earth, Mars, Jupiter, Saturn, Uranus, Neptune, and Pluto.

Number the events in the correct order.

_____ Mark painted the planets.

_____ Mark labeled the planets.

_____ Mark poked sticks into the big yellow ball.

_____ Mark looked at books to find pictures of the planets.

_____ Mark painted a Styrofoam ball
yellow to look like the sun.

_____ Mark selected Styrofoam balls in different sizes.

Whale Watching

Yesterday, Pedro's class went on a whale-watching trip. When they arrived at school, they boarded a bus that took them to Monterey Bay. Once there, they climbed aboard a large tour boat. The boat captain asked each child to put on a life vest before the boat set sail.

As the boat began to journey out onto the open sea, the tour guide told the students about the kind of animals they were likely to see on their trip. She encouraged the students to ask questions and to watch for signs of marine life.

About an hour into the trip, Pedro and his friend, Jeff, spotted a group of dolphins swimming together. The tour guide told the students that these dolphins were called Pacific white-sided dolphins. Just a short time later, they were all surprised when a large gray whale came to the surface of the water and blew air out of its large blowhole, spraying water onto the side of the boat. The students roared with laughter and excitement.

Fill in the blanks.

1. Pedro's class went whale watching in _____ Bay.

2. The _____ asked the students to put on their life vests.

3. After an hour, Pedro and _____ saw a group of dolphins.

4. The students were surprised to see a large gray _____.

5. The whale came to the _____ of the water.

6. The whale blew air out of its _____.

7. The students were overcome with excitement and _____.

Blue Jeans

There is probably no other type of clothing more popular than blue jeans. In the past century, blue jeans have become an all-American style and an important part of daily fashion. However, their creator, Levi Strauss, did not start out to make a fashion statement.

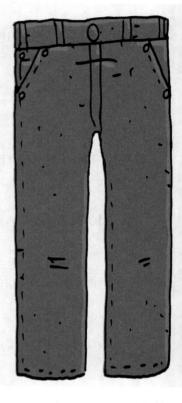

In the early 1850s, people began moving west to the state of California in search of gold. Strauss, who was a dry-goods dealer, followed this group of people in hopes of selling them tent canvas. He quickly realized that, because the people were on their knees all day panning for gold, they needed durable pants much more than they needed tents. So, Strauss turned his tent canvas material into pairs of sturdy overalls and began to make a profit!

For the next ten years, Strauss experimented with the fabric and design of his new product. First, he switched the fabric from tent canvas to sturdy French cotton called *serge de Nimes*, now known as "denim." Then, he added metal rivets, or fasteners, to make the pants stronger. Finally, he dyed the fabric a dark, indigo blue. Even today, the changes Strauss made continue to be used in the brand of blue jeans known as Levi's.

Number the events in the correct order.

_____ Strauss realized that people needed sturdy pants more than tent canvas.

_____ Strauss changed the fabric from canvas to denim and added blue dye.

_____ Strauss followed a group of people to California to sell them tent canvas.

_____ Strauss's blue jeans are known as Levi's today.

_____ Strauss made overalls out of tent canvas and sold them to people.

Science Fair

Samantha had worked for weeks on her project for the school science fair. Together, she and her father popped many bags of popcorn kernels, trying to find out which brand of kernels popped the best. It had been fun working on the project, but it was hard work, too. Along with doing the experiment over and over again, Samantha recorded data and carefully made graphs and charts to show her findings. Then, she put the information on a large sheet of sturdy poster board.

Now, as the judges approached, Samantha stood nervously in front of her project display. She held her breath as they looked at her poster and read the conclusion to her project. The judges nodded their heads and smiled at Samantha. Then, they turned to each other and huddled together, talking in quiet whispers. When they finished whispering, one of the judges presented Samantha with a blue ribbon. Samantha beamed with pride. Her hard work had paid off!

Number the events in the correct order.

—————— The judges approached Samantha's science fair project.

—————— Samantha and her dad popped popcorn kernels.

—————— Samantha received a blue ribbon.

—————— The judges read Samantha's conclusion.

—————— Samantha recorded data and made graphs and charts.

—————— The judges nodded their heads and smiled at Samantha.

The Grand Canyon

Carved by the flowing waters of the Colorado River over the last six million years, the Grand Canyon is a natural wonder. Located in northern Arizona, this amazing rocky canyon is an average of one mile deep and 277 miles long. The Grand Canyon was named a forest reserve by President Benjamin Harrison. Later, President Theodore Roosevelt declared the area to be a National Monument. Finally, in 1919, the Grand Canyon was established as a National Park.

The Grand Canyon National Park, which welcomes visitors year-round, is an excellent place to visit with your family. There are many ways to explore your surroundings, from hiking along the trails to riding on the back of a mule to the bottom of the canyon. You can also see natural land formations or, if you are lucky, catch a glimpse of rare wildlife such as the California condor or the Mexican spotted owl. Any way you spend your time at the Grand Canyon, you are likely to enjoy the natural beauty of the area.

Answer the questions.

1. Which river carved the Grand Canyon?

   _____

2. In which state is the Grand Canyon?

   _____

3. Which U.S. President established the Grand Canyon as a

   National Monument?_____

4. When was the Grand Canyon declared a National Park?

   _____

5. What is one rare animal that you might see at the Grand Canyon?

   _____

6. What are two things that you could do while visiting the Grand

   Canyon?_____

   _____

Vegetable Garden

Last spring, Emily and her brother, Jonathan, planted a vegetable garden. First, they selected a corner of their backyard and placed stakes around the area to mark the edge of the garden. Then, Jonathan raked the soil, while Emily pulled weeds out of the ground. Together, they planted a row of tomato seeds and two rows of cucumber seeds.

Every day, Jonathan and Emily checked on the garden. They watered the garden at least four times a week. Slowly, the seeds turned into sprouts, and the sprouts became plants. After weeks of waiting, vegetables began to emerge from the plants. They pulled the ripe tomatoes and cucumbers off the vine and brought them inside to eat. Emily and Jonathan were very proud of the vegetables they had grown together.

Number the events in the correct order.

_____ Jonathan raked the soil while Emily
pulled weeds out of the ground.

_____ They watered the garden four times a week.

_____ Jonathan and Emily planted a row of tomato seeds.

_____ They marked the edge of the garden.

_____ They pulled the ripe tomatoes and cucumbers
off the vine.

_____ Emily and Jonathan were very proud.

Dream Catchers

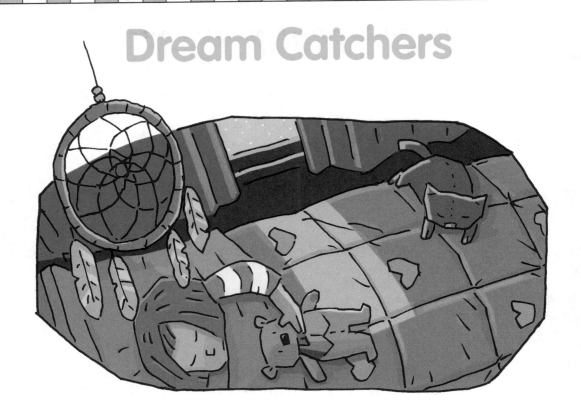

For many generations, some tribes of Native Americans have made dream catchers for their children. Today, dream catchers are usually made of willow wood wrapped in leather string. These charms look like beautiful spiders' webs. Usually hung over a child's bed, a dream catcher is said to "trap" harmful dreams at night so that bad thoughts will not disturb the sleeping child. A feather is placed in the center of the dream catcher to stand for air, which is so important for life. Other decorative pieces are often added to the dream catcher as signs for rain, beauty, or blessings. Today, many Native American people continue this custom by giving dream catchers to their loved ones.

Read each statement. Write true or false.

1. Dream catchers are an African-American tradition. _____

2. Dream catchers are made of willow wood
   and leather. _____

3. The web of the dream catcher is said to
   "trap" spiders. _____

4. The feather on the dream catcher stands for air. _____

5. Other decorative pieces are signs for rain, beauty,
   or blessings. _____

6. People do not use dream catchers today. _____

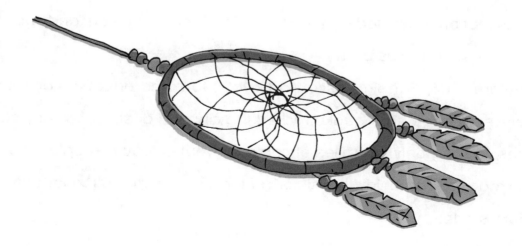

Cable Cars

Cable cars are a form of transportation created by Andrew Hallidie in the late 1800s. After noticing that it was difficult for horses to make it up and down the steep hills of San Francisco, Hallidie invented a system of cables that are operated underground. The idea caught on, and soon the cable car system was born.

Before 1906, San Francisco had over 100 miles of cable car routes. However, a large earthquake rocked the city and destroyed many of the routes, leaving only ten miles of cable car routes today. People who visit San Francisco can enjoy this historical form of transportation for only two dollars a ride!

Read each statement. Write true or false.

1. The cable car system was invented by
   Andrew Hallidie.   _____

2. Cable cars were invented in 1960.   _____

3. It was difficult for horses to make it up and
   down steep hills.   _____

4. San Francisco had a large earthquake in 1906.   _____

5. There are over 100 miles of cable car routes
   in San Francisco today.   _____

Making the Team

Vincent decided that he needed to get in better shape if he wanted to make the track team. Every morning, he woke up a half-hour early. He put on his running shoes and headed out the door. He ran for two miles each morning before school. Every day, it took him less time than the day before. Soon, Vincent was running faster and more easily than ever before.

On the day of track team tryouts, his friend Greg asked Vincent if he was ready. Vincent nodded his head nervously and took his mark on the track. At the sound of the coach's whistle, Vincent took off! He ran as fast and as steadily as he could. As he finished his second lap around the track, the coach clicked his stopwatch. He looked down at the time, then smiled at Vincent and said, "Congratulations!"

Number the events in the correct order.

Then answer the question below.

_____ Vincent's friend asked him if he was ready.

_____ Vincent finished his second lap around the track.

_____ The coach smiled at Vincent.

_____ Vincent ran for two miles every morning.

_____ At the sound of the whistle, Vincent took off.

_____ Vincent decided that he wanted to try out for the track team.

Do you think Vincent made the track team? Explain.

_____

_____

Avalanche!

An avalanche is a large clump of snow sliding down a mountain. Avalanches happen mostly between the months of January and March. Most fall during or just after large snowstorms. The most common starting point of an avalanche is on a slope of 30-45 degrees. On the top of the slope, snow will form and create a snow cover. As the pull of gravity grows stronger, the snow becomes unstable. This causes the release of pressure that begins the avalanche. As it comes down the mountain, more snow is added and it picks up speed. An avalanche is dangerous because it can happen with little warning, burying everything in its path.

Read each statement. Write true or false.

1. Avalanches happen between June and August. _____

2. Most avalanches fall during or just after a snowstorm. _____

3. Avalanches often start on slopes of 65-80 degrees. _____

4. The pull of gravity often causes snow cover
   to be unstable. _____

5. An avalanche can occur with little warning. _____

6. An avalanche is not dangerous if you know how to ski. _____

Puzzles

Jim loves putting puzzles together. The greater the number of pieces in the puzzle, the more challenging and fun it is for him. So far, Jim has assembled puzzles showing pictures of a hot-air balloon, a race car, a space shuttle, and a library bookshelf. Each puzzle Jim solves is harder than the last.

For his birthday, Jim's sister gave him a 3-D puzzle with 3,500 pieces in it. It has a picture of a globe on the outside of the box. Once Jim figures out how to fit all the pieces together, the puzzle will make a round model of the world! Jim can't wait to get started.

Answer the questions.

1. What does Jim love to do?

   _____

2. What makes puzzles more challenging to Jim?

   _____

3. What are three pictures that Jim's puzzles have made?

   _____

4. Who gave Jim a puzzle for his birthday?

   _____

5. How many pieces did the puzzle have in it?

   _____

6. After Jim assembles the 3-D puzzle, what shape will it make?

   _____

Piano Lessons

Mrs. Appleton teaches piano lessons to eight students on Oakwood Street. Each student has one half-hour lesson a week. Mrs. Appleton teaches them how to read music and shows them how to play scales. This helps the students learn how to play different music on the piano.

At the end of the year, Mrs. Appleton hosts a recital for the students. Each student selects a song to play. They practice and practice the songs until they are ready to play in front of an audience. Then, each student invites his or her friends and family to watch the recital. Mrs. Appleton is always very pleased with the efforts of her students.

Answer the questions.

1. On which street does Mrs. Appleton teach piano lessons?

   _____

2. How many students does Mrs. Appleton teach?

   _____

3. What does Mrs. Appleton host at the end of the year?

   _____

4. Who is invited to the recital?

   _____

   _____

5. How does Mrs. Appleton feel about her students' performances?

   _____

Pyramids

The ancient pyramids of Egypt were built as burial places, or tombs, for great rulers called pharaohs. The pyramids were made with large blocks of stone. These blocks were dragged across the desert by groups of men, then carefully set in place. Scientists think it took 20 years to build one of these giant buildings! Before sealing the pharaoh's tomb, the Egyptians would make carvings, paintings, and diagrams inside the walls. Along with the bodies of the pharaohs, gifts of jewels, statues, and other priceless treasures were sealed inside the pyramids. The Egyptians believed that the dead person would use these items in his next life.

Today, about 80 pyramids still exist. The three largest and most famous are in Giza, near Cairo. Scientists study these amazing buildings as examples of Egyptian culture thousands of years ago.

Fill in the blanks. Write the answers in the puzzle.

Across

2. The Pyramids were built as burial places, or _____, for pharaohs.

4. Inside the tombs, Egyptians made carvings, _____,
   and diagrams.

Down

1. The pyramids are an example of Egyptian _____.

3. Gifts of jewels and statues were _____ inside the tombs.

5. Pieces of _____ were cut and pieced together.

The Big Day

Heather laced up her skates and went over her routine in her head. She had practiced for this moment for six months. She knew she was ready. Heather took a deep breath, then slowly rose to her feet. She turned to find her mother in the crowd. Her mom smiled and waved, giving her a confident nod. Heather smiled and nodded back.

Placing one foot on the ice, Heather held her head up high and glided out to the center of the arena. As she found her place, she saw the judges out of the corner of her eye. She calmly placed one hand on her hip and the other high in the air. She dug the tip of her skate into the ice and stood very still, waiting for the music to begin. Heather knew she would give the performance of her life.

Circle the correct answer.

1. Heather was probably about to _____.

    a. perform in a skating competition

    b. perform a magic trick

    c. race across the ice

2. Heather had practiced for _____ months.

    a. seven   b. two   c. six

3. Before Heather stepped onto the ice, she saw _____.

    a. the judges   b. her mom   c. her best friend

4. When Heather stood on the ice, she was waiting for _____.

    a. her hip to feel better

    b. the crowd to cheer

    c. the music to begin

5. Based on the story, Heather was probably _____ to perform.

    a. ready   b. not ready   c. not going

6. Another good title for this story might be _____.

    a. Everyone Makes Mistakes

    b. Heather's Performance

    c. Heather's Mom

Sticker Collection

Jennifer has over 130 stickers in her sticker collection. Her stickers come in all shapes and sizes, but most are designs that show her interests. Jennifer collects flower stickers because she likes to work in the garden with her grandmother. She also collects ballet and musical note stickers because she loves to dance. She uses the stickers to decorate her folders, notebooks, and letters. Jennifer keeps her stickers safely tucked away in a plastic box underneath her bed.

Answer the questions.

1. How many stickers does Jennifer have?

   _____

2. Why does Jennifer collect flower stickers?

   _____

3. Which stickers show Jennifer's interest in dancing?

   _____

4. What does Jennifer do with her stickers?

   _____

5. Where does she keep the stickers?

   _____

A Win-Win Situation

Hannah's class had won the contest! Two weeks ago, the school principal had challenged the students to see which class could collect the most cans of food. The food would be given to a local shelter for homeless families. In addition to the good feeling they would get from helping others, the winning class was promised an ice-cream party reward.

The school was buzzing with excitement as the last day of the contest approached. One of the fifth grade classes had already collected 124 cans of food! Hannah's class fell just short of the fifth grade class, with 113 cans. On the final day of the contest, however, Hannah and her classmates brought a total of 27 cans of food, bringing their total to 140. Hannah and her friends were very excited about winning the ice-cream party, but they were also proud to have made a difference in the lives of others.

Answer the questions.

1. What was the contest at Hannah's school?

   _____

   _____

2. To whom would the cans be given after the contest was over?

   _____

   _____

3. What was the reward promised to the winning class?

   _____

4. Which class was in first place before the last day of the contest?

   _____

5. On the final day of the contest, what was the total number of cans

   collected by the winning class?_____

6. Why were Hannah's classmates proud at the end of the contest?

   _____

   _____

Book Report

Writing a book report is a great way to share books with your classmates. You should begin a book report with the title of the book and the name of the author. Then, you should briefly introduce the characters in the story. Next, you should try to tell about the events in the book, but be careful not to give away the ending.

At the conclusion of the book report, you should tell whether or not you enjoyed the book and why. By reading your book report, other students can get more information about the book and decide whether or not they would like to read it.

Read each statement. Write true or false.

1. A book report is a good way to share books with librarians. _____

2. A book report should include the name of the author. _____

3. You should not give away the ending of the book in a book report. _____

4. You should tell others why you did or did not enjoy the book. _____

5. Other students in your class are required to read the book you read. _____

Newspaper Reporters

Have you ever wondered how newspapers find information to print stories? Newspapers hire people called reporters to research information and write stories to put in the newspaper. Newspaper reporters gather information about a variety of topics. Some reporters write about sports or weather, while other reporters find out what is happening in the daily lives of people in our communities or in other countries around the world. In any case, a reporter must interview a variety of different people and ask the same basic questions to gather information. Those essential questions are: Who? What? When? Where? Why? How? Once a reporter has discovered the answer to these questions, he or she is able to write a complete story that informs the reader. These stories are printed in daily newspapers all over the world and delivered right to our doorsteps.

Answer the questions.

1. Who gathers information and writes stories for newspapers?

   _____

2. According to the passage, what are two subjects that a reporter

   might write about? _____

3. What must a reporter do when he or she interviews people?

   _____

4. What are the six essential questions a reporter must ask?

   _____

   _____

5. Why is it helpful for a reporter to discover the answers to these six

   questions? _____

   _____

Washington Monument

Open to the public in 1888, the Washington Monument was built as a memorial to George Washington, the first President of the United States. The original design of the Washington Monument was created in 1836 by an architect named Robert Mills. It included a statue of Washington in a chariot at the top of the structure. Building began on July 4, 1848, but several delays prevented work on the monument. By 1858, the start of the Civil War interrupted further construction.

After the war ended, Lieutenant Colonel Thomas L. Casey continued the project in 1876 by redesigning the monument in the shape of an obelisk, or a slender, four-sided pointed structure. His version did not contain a statue of Washington or any other figure. This tall monument is a simple yet beautiful design that stands today in Washington, D.C. as a tribute to our nation's first elected leader.

Write the event in the correct place on the time line.

The Washington Monument opens to the public.

Robert Mills creates the original design.

Thomas L. Casey redesigns the monument.

The Civil War begins.

Building of the Washington Monument begins.

1836 _____

_____

1848 _____

_____

1858 _____

_____

1876 _____

_____

1888 _____

_____

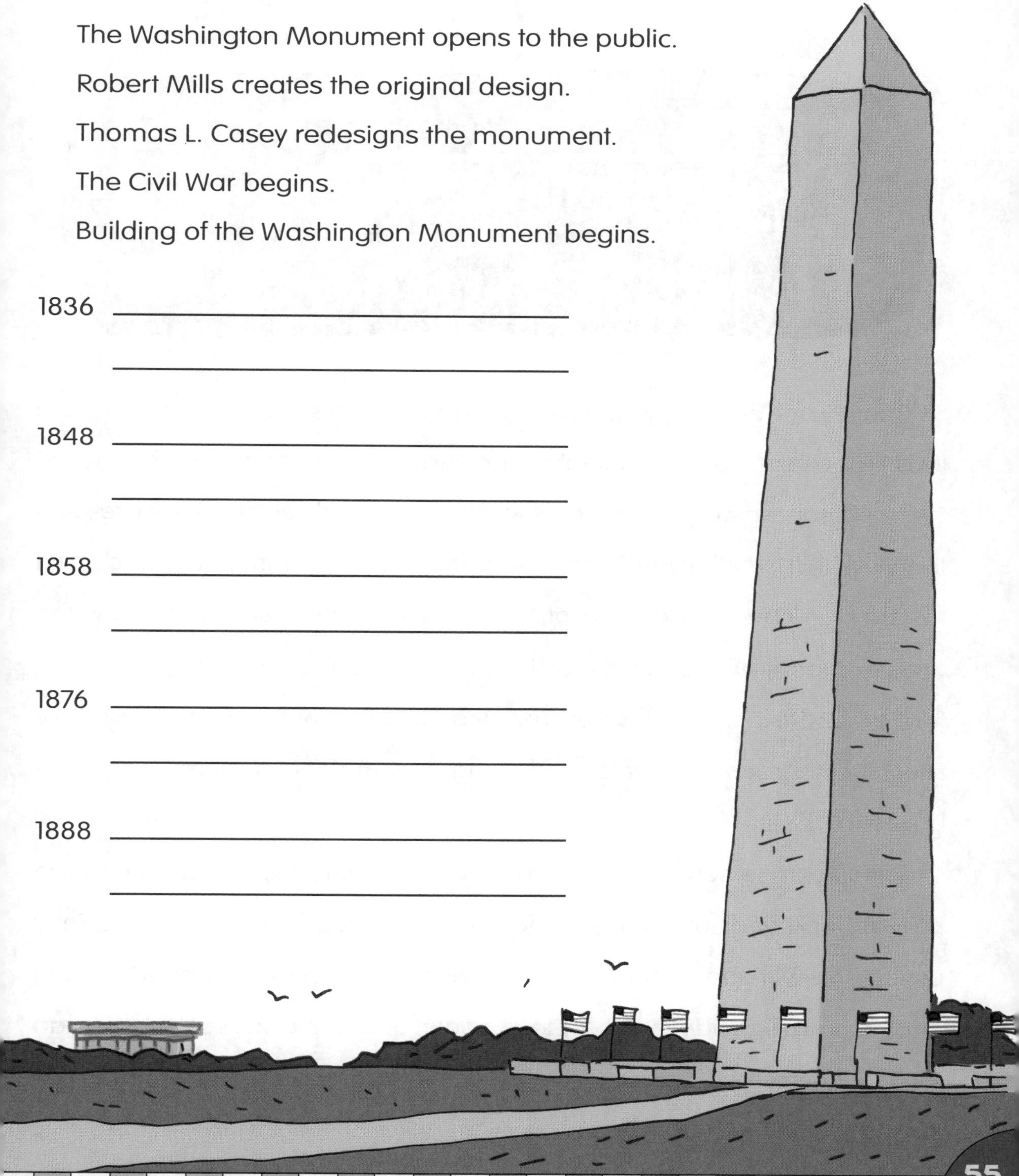

Working like a Dog

Search and rescue dogs are trained to find missing people and save lives. These special dogs use their powerful sense of smell in their work. Every person has a special scent, and search and rescue dogs are able to follow this smell, even in crowded areas. Just one trained search and rescue dog can do the work of ten trained human searchers! They can work in places where human sight is limited, such as in dark areas, thick forests, and even under water. The dogs know how to search in disaster sites, locate trapped people, and signal their trainers to show what they have found.

These canine heroes must train to keep up their skills. They go through at least one year of training before they are ready to start work. They usually live with their trainers. When their special skills are needed, search and rescue dogs ride in helicopters, boats, and airplanes so that they can rush to the scene of a rescue, just like their human coworkers!

Fill in the blanks. Write the answers in the puzzle.

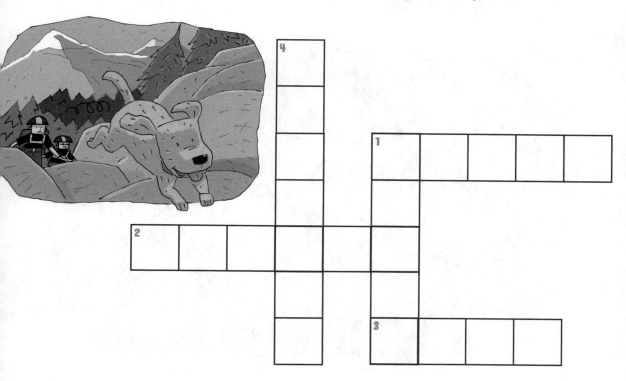

Across

1. Search and rescue dogs can work in places where human

   _____ is limited.

2. These _____ heroes must train to keep up their skills.

3. Search and rescue dogs usually _____ with their trainers.

Down

1. These special dogs use their powerful sense of _____

   in their work.

4. Search and rescue dogs are trained to find _____ people.

A Visit to the Dentist

Robert waited patiently outside the dentist's office. A dental assistant called Robert's name, and he looked up at her. Robert's mother patted him on the shoulder and told Robert to follow the lady into the office.

At first, Robert was a little nervous, but the dental assistant smiled kindly and told him that there was nothing to worry about. Once inside the office, Robert sat down in the dental chair. The assistant hooked a bib around Robert's neck. Then she used fluoride and a tooth polisher to clean Robert's teeth. Next, the dentist came in and took X-rays of Robert's teeth. The dentist told Robert that his teeth and gums looked very healthy. Robert smiled proudly and left the dentist's office.

Answer the questions.

1. Who called Robert into the dentist's office?

   _____

2. Who was waiting with Robert outside the dentist's office?

   _____

3. How was Robert feeling as he entered the dentist's office?

   _____

4. What are two things that were used to clean Robert's teeth?

   _____

   _____

5. What news did the dentist tell Robert?

   _____

   _____

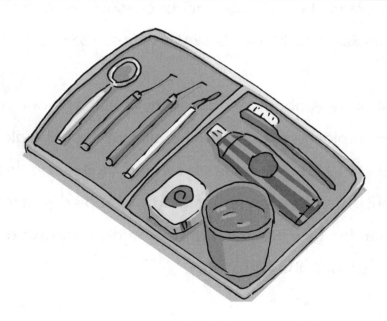

Keshon's New Bike

Keshon pressed his nose against the glass of the store window for the third time this week. He stared longingly at the shiny red bike with a white racing stripe. As always, the blue price tag seemed to scream loudly at him, "Only $59.99!" At times, Keshon remembered thinking that the sign may as well say "One Million Dollars!" Either way, he did not have the money to buy it.

Today, however, was different. Keshon took his wallet out of his hip pocket and counted the bills he had been saving from mowing the lawns of neighbors on his block. He slowly counted $56.75. Soon, the bike would be his!

Just as Keshon was about to walk away, the store manager came to the window. He replaced the sign on the bike with a red "sale" sign! The new price was $54.99. Keshon jumped in the air. He ran into the store with excitement. The store manager gladly accepted Keshon's money and handed him the bike. Keshon hopped on his new bike and headed home, grinning proudly the whole way.

Answer the questions.

1. Why was Keshon pressing his nose against the glass of the store window?_____

   _____

2. What did the bike look like?

   _____

3. How much money had Keshon saved?

   _____

4. How did Keshon earn the money?

   _____

5. What was the price that Keshon paid for the bike?

   _____

Page 5
1. opening day of the major-league baseball season
2. The President of the United States
3. April 4, 1910
4. William Howard Taft
5. Philadelphia and Washington

Page 7
1. "Star-Spangled Banner"
2. Francis Scott Key
3. 1812
4. 1900s
5. 1931

Page 9
1. spelling bees
2. in the late 1700s
3. Benjamin Franklin
4. parents, friends, and neighbors
5. quilting bees and corn-husking bees

Page 11
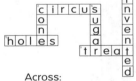

Across:
  2. circus
  4. holes
  5. treat
Down:
  1. invented
  2. cone

Page 13
1. false
2. true
3. false
4. true
5. true

Page 15
These statements should be circled:
Dolphins are mammals.
Dolphins use echolocation to find food.
Dolphins "talk" to each other using clicking sounds

Page 17
1. adults
2. June 6, 1933
3. Richard M. Hollingshead, Jr.
4. 25¢
5. Now it's something everyone can enjoy.

Page 19
3 Mark painted the planets.
6 Mark labeled the planets.
5 Mark poked sticks into the big yellow ball.
2 Mark looked at books to find pictures of the planets.
4 Mark painted a Styrofoam ball yellow to look like the sun.
1 Mark selected Styrofoam balls in different sizes.

Page 21
1. Monterey
2. captain
3. Jeff
4. whale

5. surface
6. blowhole
7. laughter

Page 23
2 Strauss realized that people needed sturdy pants more than tent canvas.
4 Strauss changed the fabric from canvas to denim and added blue dye.
1 Strauss followed a group of people to California to sell them tent canvas.
5 Strauss's blue jeans are known as Levi's today.
3 Strauss made overalls out of tent canvas and sold them to people.

Page 25
3 The judges approached Samantha's science fair project.
1 Samantha and her dad popped popcorn kernels.
6 Samantha received a blue ribbon.
4 The judges read Samantha's conclusion.
2 Samantha recorded data and made graphs and charts.
5 The judges nodded their heads and smiled at Samantha.

Page 27
1. Colorado River
2. Arizona
3. Theodore Roosevelt

4. 1919
5. Answer will be either California condor or Mexican spotted owl.
6. Answer should include things like hiking, riding mules, seeing land formations, or watching wildlife.

Page 29
2 Jonathan raked the soil while Emily pulled weeds out of the ground.
4 They watered the garden four times a week.
3 Jonathan and Emily planted a row of tomato seeds.
1 They marked the edge of the garden.
5 They pulled the ripe tomatoes and cucumbers off the vine.
6 Emily and Jonathan were very proud.

Page 31
1. false
2. true
3. false
4. true
5. true
6. false

Page 33
1. true
2. false
3. true
4. true
5. false

Answer Key

Page 35
3 Vincent's friend asked him if he was ready.
5 Vincent finished his second lap around the track.
6 The coach smiled at Vincent.
2 Vincent ran for two miles every morning.
4 At the sound of the whistle, Vincent took off.
1 Vincent decided that he wanted to try out for the track team.

Answers to final question will vary.

Page 37
1. false
2. true
3. false
4. true
5. true
6. false

Page 39
1. He loves to put puzzles together.
2. more pieces
3. Answer should include three of the following: hot-air balloon, race car, space shuttle, or bookshelf.
4. Jim's sister
5. 3,500 pieces
6. It will make a round model of the world.

Page 41
1. Oakwood Street
2. eight

3. a recital
4. the students and friends and family
5. She is pleased.

Page 43

```
        c
 t o m b s u
      e   l
 p a i n t i n g s
      l   u     t
      e   r     o
      d   e     n
                e
```

Across:
   2. tombs
   4. paintings
Down:
   1. culture
   3. sealed
   5. stone

Page 45
1. a. perform in a skating competition
2. c. six
3. b. her mom
4. c. the music to begin
5. a. ready
6. b. Heather's Performance

Page 47
1. over 130
2. She likes to work in the garden with her grandmother.
3. ballet and musical note stickers
4. She uses them to decorate folders, notebooks, and letters.
5. in a plastic box underneath her bed

Page 49
1. It was a contest

to see which class could collect the most cans of food.
2. a local shelter for homeless families
3. an ice-cream party
4. a fifth grade class
5. 140
6. They were proud to have made a difference in the lives of others.

Page 51
1. false
2. true
3. true
4. true
5. false

Page 53
1. newspaper reporters
2. Answer should include two of the following: sports, weather, daily lives in the community or around the world.
3. ask questions
4. who? what? when? where? why? how?
5. so that the reporter can accurately inform the reader

Page 55
1836 • Robert Mills creates the original design.
1848 • Building of the Washington Monument begins.
1858 • The Civil War begins.
1876 • Thomas L. Casey redesigns

the monument.
1888 • The Washington Monument opens to the public.

Page 57

```
        m
        i
        s   s i g h t
        s   m
 c a n i n e
        n   l
        g   l i v e
```

Across:
   1. sight
   2. canine
   3. live
Down:
   1. smell
   4. missing

Page 59
1. the dental assistant
2. Robert's mom
3. a little nervous
4. fluoride and a tooth polisher
5. His teeth and gums look healthy

Page 61
1. He was looking at a new bike.
2. It was red with a white racing stripe.
3. $56.75
4. He mowed lawns of neighbors on his block.
5. $54.99

63

Great Job!